YOU AND YOUR PET
AQUARIUM
PETS

YOU AND YOUR PET
AQUARIUM PETS

PHIL STEINBERG

Illustrations by CHRISTINE A. WOLD

Lerner Publications Company
Minneapolis

Front cover photo by Pierre Michel Rapho. © 1974 by Librairie A. Hatier.
Back cover photo by Klaus Paysan.

LIBRARY OF CONGRESS CATALOGING IN PUBLICATION DATA

Steinberg, Phillip Orso.
  Aquarium pets.

  (You and Your Pet)
  Includes index.
  SUMMARY: Information on setting up an aquarium and on
various plants and animals one might choose to inhabit it.

  1. Aquariums—Juvenile literature. [1. Aquariums] I. Wold,
Christine A. II. Title. III. Series.

SF457.25.S86 1979   639'.34   78-54359
ISBN 0-8225-1255-6

Manufactured in the United States of America. Published
simultaneously in Canada by J. M. Dent & Sons (Canada) Ltd.,
Don Mills, Ontario.

International Standard Book Number: 0-8225-1255-6
Library of Congress Catalog Card Number: 78-54359

2 3 4 5 6 7 8 9 10 85 84 83 82 81 80

CONTENTS

Underwater Life   7

About Fish   9

The Importance of Oxygen
    to Underwater Life   12

Setting Up a Fresh-Water Aquarium   16

Planting an Underwater Garden   24

Putting Fish in Your Tank   27

Snails   30

Keeping the Aquarium Clean   31

Feeding Your Fish   33

Fresh-Water Exotics   35

Salt-Water Aquariums   46

Marine Creatures   50

Index   54

UNDERWATER LIFE

The beauty of crystal-clear water, lush green plants, and rainbow-colored fish has made aquarium keeping a popular hobby for more than 20 million Americans. Those who keep aquariums are able to observe and enjoy the underwater world right in their homes or schools.

Aquarium keeping is not a new hobby, however. Wealthy Romans often built shallow pools in their homes and stocked them with colorful fish. And the ancient Chinese and Japanese developed the goldfish from a dull green variety into the colorful, fancy-finned varieties found in pet stores today.

More important than the beauty of exotic fish is the knowledge they give us. Most scientists believe the sea to be the cradle of life. They theorize that life originated in the sea, starting with tiny one-celled organisms. Then, about 500 million years ago fish appeared. They were the first animals to have backbones. Since that time, land creatures, including humans, have evolved. But even today, the sea harbors the greatest variety of life, just as in earliest times. Because the sea provides such a variety of life and because it probably will be the chief source of human food someday, aquarium keeping is more than just a pleasurable hobby. It is a way of studying the intricate balance of underwater life, on which people are becoming increasingly dependent.

Making a small glass tank of water as much like an ocean, lake, or pond as possible is, indeed, a challenge. Before you take your first step toward setting up an aquarium, you should realize what hard work keeping fish really is. Much time is required for setting up and maintaining an aquarium. The fish you put in the tank will rely on you for their food and the proper water conditions to keep them healthy. They cannot live without your faithful attention. If you are willing to make the effort and to spend the time on an aquarium, you are in for hours of fun and fascination. You are on your way to becoming an *aquarist*, a person who keeps an aquarium.

Most people who keep aquariums call their fish "tropicals." The reason for this is that many aquarium fish come from the warm, tropical regions of the world. Not all aquarium fish, however, come from the tropics.

Whale Shark

Goldfish, for example, are native to the temperate areas of China and Japan. It is best, then, to refer to all aquarium fish as "exotic" fish. By "exotic," we mean any aquarium fish that is beautiful or unusual in appearance, or any fish that has curious habits — regardless of the region from which it comes.

ABOUT FISH

To care for fish, you should know something about them. Roughly 21,000 kinds of fish have been named and described, and more are being discovered every year. They range in size from the half-inch (1.25-centimeter) pygmy goby of the Philippines to the whale shark, which can reach a length of 60 feet (18 meters).

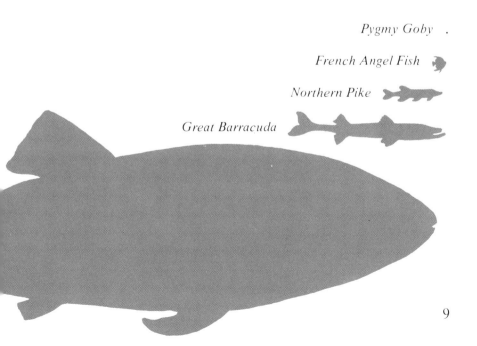

Pygmy Goby

French Angel Fish

Northern Pike

Great Barracuda

Fish are found in all parts of the world. Some species live in the dark depths of the ocean—as far down as seven miles. Others live in lightless caves and underground rivers. Still others can be found in alpine streams 15,000 feet (4,500 meters) above sea level. And others live in the cold waters of the Arctic Ocean. Some even thrive in natural hot springs that reach temperatures of 110 degrees Fahrenheit (43 degrees Celsius).

Fish are cold-blooded, which means they cannot regulate their body temperatures. Instead, they assume the temperature of their surroundings. The blood in a fish's system is circulated by a simple two-chambered heart; blood is collected in one chamber and pumped through the body by the other.

Fish are vertebrates, which means they have backbones. Most fish have skeletons composed mainly of bone. But some fish, such as sharks and rays, have skeletons composed of cartilage (KAR-tih-lihj), a tough, elastic substance.

Fish reproduce in two basic ways. Some species bear their young alive and are called "live-bearers." And some fish lay eggs. Most "egg-layers" have to lay thousands and thousands of eggs for even a few young to hatch and grow to adulthood.

When you tell a friend that he or she "swims like a fish," you are giving a compliment, because most fish swim very well. The great sailfish and swordfish can swim at speeds of more than 30 miles (48 kilometers) an

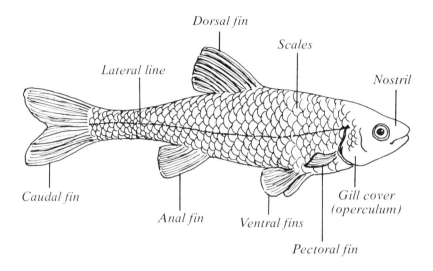

Dorsal fin
Scales
Lateral line
Nostril
Caudal fin
Anal fin
Ventral fins
Gill cover (operculum)
Pectoral fin

hour. The mackerel moves at about 7 miles (11.2 kilometers) an hour, which is three times faster than the rate at which people move on land. Even the tiny guppy can swim half a mile (0.8 kilometer) in an hour.

In addition to swimming, some fish fly or walk. The California flying fish can leap into the air and glide as if it were flying. Examples of fish that walk are the climbing perch, the mudspringer, and the rockskipper. "Walking fish" support themselves on strong pelvic fins and move as people on crutches move. Certain land-going fish have special organs in their heads that make it possible for them to take oxygen directly from the air. They can live in or out of water. Most fish, however, take oxygen from the water through the *gills*, membranes rich in blood vessels.

Fish have a good sense of smell. They use this sense for finding food, locating home territories, and detecting enemies. For hearing and balance, fish are equipped with simple inner ears. They also have a special sense called the "lateral line system." This system is made up of tiny pores, or holes, along the fish's head and sides that are very sensitive to movements and vibrations. The lateral line system helps the fish to locate food or to detect danger.

THE IMPORTANCE OF OXYGEN TO UNDERWATER LIFE

The idea behind keeping an aquarium is to create an environment for fish as much like their natural home as possible. Exotic fish, as well as humans and other animals, need clean living spaces, proper food, and oxygen (OX-ih-jen). Perhaps you have noticed how fish keep opening and closing their mouths as if chewing. What they are really doing is breathing. They breathe by drawing water into their mouths and passing it over a series of tiny blood vessels in the gills. Gills are rows of red fringes in the slits at the sides of a fish's head. In some ways gills act like lungs. The gills take oxygen out of the water just as lungs take oxygen out of the air. Animals need oxygen in their cells to change food into energy.

When there is not enough oxygen in aquarium water,

the fish will swim near the top of the tank and gulp for air. This is a call for help, a warning that the fish are suffocating. A lack of oxygen is caused either by too many fish in the tank or by poor water conditions. If this condition is not corrected the fish will die.

The air that supplies oxygen to the fish is absorbed at the water's surface. Because most aquariums do not have enough water surface to supply all the oxygen that fish need, the supply of oxygen must be increased by means of plants and mechanical devices.

As fish breathe, they take in oxygen and give off carbon dioxide (KAR-buhn die-OX-ide). This process of adding oxygen to the blood and removing carbon dioxide is called *respiration* and is carried on by all animals. Growing plants, however, perform a sort of reverse of this cycle. They absorb carbon dioxide and give off oxygen. Thus, plants use up carbon dioxide harmful to fish and also produce some of the oxygen necessary for animal respiration.

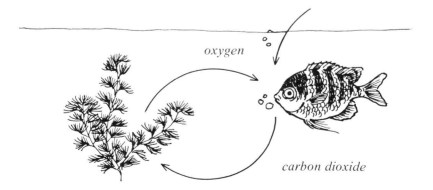

oxygen

carbon dioxide

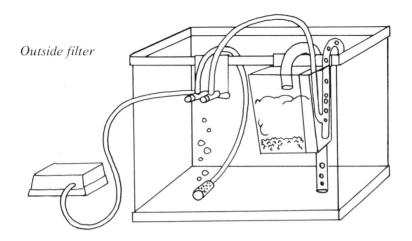

Outside filter

An *aerator* (AIR-a-tor) supplies the bulk of the oxygen that aquarium fish need. It is operated by a little electric machine that blows air into the water, making hundreds of tiny bubbles. These bubbles gently move the water, helping it to give up carbon dioxide and take on oxygen. There are many different kinds of aerators, some of which are designed to work in the same system as a filter.

A *filter* is a very important part of every aquarium. It helps to clear the water of old food and fish waste, thus keeping your fish healthy and preventing bad smells in the aquarium. As with aerators, there are many different kinds of filters. Some filters are located outside the tank. The aquarium water is pumped through them with little electric motors. Other filters are located in the tank, right in the water.

A most effective in-the-tank filter is the under-gravel system. This system uses the aquarium gravel as a sort of filter, sucking the water down through the gravel. As the water is pulled through the gravel, it brings debris with it. The fish waste and old food that are pulled into the gravel decompose and become fertilizer for the aquarium plants. The water that passes through the gravel is cleansed and goes up through a tube, out into the aquarium again. The filtered water aerates the aquarium as it enters the tank. As you can see, the under-gravel system both filters and aerates the water in one operation.

There are many different kinds of aerating and filtering systems. Before you buy aquarium equipment, look at all the systems in a pet store and be sure to ask a lot of questions about each one. Learn the effectiveness of each system and its price. Be sure to get a system that will take care of the size aquarium you want, and get instructions on how to operate your system and care for it.

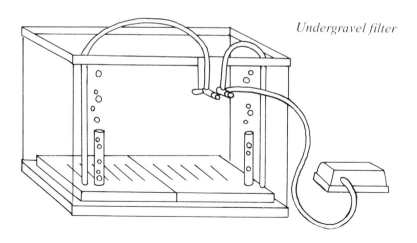

Undergravel filter

SETTING UP A FRESH-WATER AQUARIUM

Of the hundreds of thousands of water creatures, small, exotic fish are the ones that will be discussed in this book. They can be divided into two general categories—salt-water fish and fresh-water fish. Among the fresh-water varieties, there are fish native to tropical climates and also those used to temperate climates. For each group you must set up a different kind of aquarium. Cool-water tanks are good for displaying goldfish. Warm-water tanks are good for showing off the striking tropical varieties. And salt-water tanks are reserved for fish native to the ocean.

Setting up an aquarium means lots of hard work even before you buy the fish. If you take time to do everything in the proper order, your fish will be healthy and they will live longer.

In setting up an aquarium, the first thing to do is to pick out a fish tank. Tanks vary in size from 5 gallons to 100 gallons. The small 5-gallon tanks are not intended as community tanks but usually are used for breeding purposes or for housing sick fish. It is best to start with the biggest tank you can afford. It should hold at least 10 gallons of water, but a 20-gallon tank is ideal. A completely equipped 20-gallon tank that is ready for fish costs about $35. Smaller tanks and equipment cost almost as much, so you may as well buy the larger tank.

Large tanks have many advantages over small tanks. They are easier to keep in good condition. Water

temperature does not vary as much in a large tank. The water stays clean longer. Plants grow better in a large tank. And the fish have more room in which to swim; fish crowded into a small tank tend to be unfriendly. The best reason for having a large tank is that you can keep more fish in it.

Several kinds of tanks are available in pet shops. Some are made of plastic, others are made of glass plates held together by metal frames, and still others are constructed entirely of glass. The all-glass tanks are best because they will not leak. And they are the only tanks you can use for salt-water aquariums.

Your aquarium must be supported in some way. Place it on a strong table or rest it on an aquarium stand. Because water is heavy, the table or stand you use should be very sturdy. A 20-gallon tank full of water weighs more than 165 pounds (about 74 kilograms). Aquarium stands make the best supports because they are made of metal. They come in sizes to fit every tank, and the average cost is about $20.

Once you have decided upon the size and kind of tank, you must find a place for it before you fill it with water. (The aquarium should be moved only when empty—moving a full tank may cause it to leak.) Do not place your stand and tank in front of a window, because daylight will cause *algae* (AL-gee) to grow. Algae are tiny plants that can turn the water green. But because other aquarium plants need light to grow, you will need to install a reflector with electric lights in it. (Algae generally does not grow well under artificial light.) The fluorescent light tubes sold in most pet shops show off the colors of the fish and encourage other plant growth if left on eight to ten hours every day.

A reflector covers only part of the top of the aquarium, so you will need a thick plate of glass to cover the rest of the opening. This glass cover will keep out dust and prevent your fish from leaping out of the tank.

An aquarium hood is even better than a reflector and glass. It covers the entire top of the tank and has built-in sockets for electric lights. Hoods cost more but are worth the difference in price. Your hood or reflector should be placed so that the light shines toward the back of the tank. This arrangement will show off your fish to better advantage.

To keep other sources of light from flooding into the back of the tank, paint the back of your aquarium on the outside. This job requires a special paint called "aquarium crystal paint." As the paint dries, it forms crystal patterns on the glass that are lovely when viewed through water. Though crystal paint comes in many colors, the most sea-like color is medium green. Crystal paint can be applied with a brush or sprayed directly onto the glass.

Fish are cold-blooded animals. This means that a fish's body temperature is nearly the same as the temperature of the water in which it lives. For this reason, aquarium water must constantly be maintained at the proper temperature. For tropical and salt-water fish, the water should be between 72 and 75 degrees Fahrenheit (22 to 24 degrees Celsius). The water temperature can be kept constant through use of a thermostat-heater. This is an electric tube that hangs in the aquarium. By turning a little knob on the top of the heater, you can control the temperature.

You should keep a floating thermometer in your tank and check it twice a day. If the water temperature falls below 72 degrees, turn the knob on the heater forward a bit. If the temperature rises above 75 degrees, turn the knob back a bit. Water temperature should be changed gradually. Any sudden change in water temperature could make your fish ill or kill them.

Because goldfish come from a temperate climate, they thrive in water temperatures between 50 and 68 degrees Fahrenheit (10 and 20 degrees Celsius). Therefore, you do not need a heater for a goldfish tank.

Now that you have selected your tank and a place for it, you must clean it carefully. Do not use glass cleaner or soap on the inside of the tank; chemicals in the

cleaner and soap are harmful to fish. A pail of water with about four tablespoons of table salt in it makes an excellent cleaner. Slosh the salt water around the glass and then rinse the tank thoroughly with clear water. Rinse the tank several times to remove all the salt. Your tank is now ready for gravel.

There is a special kind of gravel, or crushed rock, made for aquariums. It comes in many colors and sizes, the best size being a medium grade number 2 or 3. Natural gravel looks best in a well-planted aquarium; colored gravel tends to detract from the fish and plants. Be sure that the gravel you use is especially made for aquariums. Never use sand.

You will need enough gravel to cover the tank's bottom to a depth of 1¾ inches (3.75 centimeters) in the front and 2 inches (5 centimeters) in the back. You will need about 30 pounds (13.5 kilograms) of gravel for a 20-gallon tank. Fish-tank gravel is not expensive.

Before putting the gravel in, you must wash it. To do this, put about 10 pounds (4.5 kilograms) of gravel in a plastic pail and fill it with water. Stir the gravel with a wooden stick until the dirt and dust come to the surface. Pour off the dirty water. Repeat this process until the gravel rinses clean.

If you have an under-gravel filter, place it on the bottom of the tank before adding the gravel. Then spread the gravel so that it slopes from the back of the tank to the front.

Now you are ready to put in ornaments. Sunken ships, little bridges, and rocks add an interesting touch to your aquarium. Do not use rocks and ornaments that dissolve in the water, because the dissolved particles could poison the fish. It is safer to use ornaments that are sold in pet shops.

Your tank is now ready for water. Place a few sheets of newspaper on top of the gravel and slowly pour water into the tank until it is filled to within half an inch (1.25 centimeters) of the top. The newspaper will keep the pouring water from digging holes in the gravel and stirring it up. After you are finished pouring, remove the newspaper.

The water in the tank must age about four or five days before plants and fish can be added. City water is

22

treated with chemicals, including chlorine, that make it safe for people to drink. But these chemicals will kill tropical fish. Aging water allows the chemicals to settle out, making the water safe for plants and fish. Pet shops sell a liquid that removes chlorine from water almost immediately, but aging the water is safer. After the water has aged in the tank, you may begin planting your underwater garden.

Salvinia   *Riccia*   *Duckweed*

PLANTING AN UNDERWATER GARDEN

Plants not only contribute oxygen to your aquarium but also add beauty to the tank and provide hiding places for small fish. Dozens of different aquarium plants, divided into three main groups, are available in pet shops. *Rooted plants* are planted directly in the gravel. One of the most popular rooted plants is the Amazon sword plant. Its lovely foliage will be the center of interest in your underwater garden. Other popular rooted plants are sagittaria, corkscrew, banana plant, and eel grass.

The second group, known as *bunched plants*, is sold in bunches tied at the bottom and weighted. Cabomba, anacharis, and water sprite are examples of bunched plants.

Floating plants float on top of the water. They provide hiding places for very young fish. But because they prevent light from reaching the bottom of the tank, they should be used sparingly. Salvinia, riccia, and duckweed are examples of floating plants.

Anacharis

Cabomba

Water Sprite

Sagittaria

Amazon Swordplant

Corkscrew

Eelgrass

Banana Plant

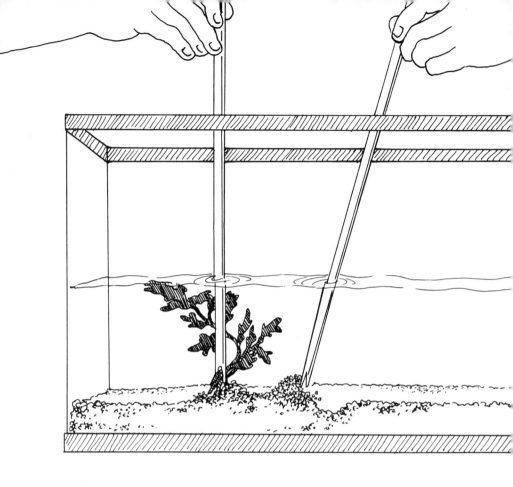

Before planting the aquarium, be sure to wash all
your plants under the faucet to remove any insects,
snails, and eggs that may be sticking to the leaves.
Removing a pail or two of water from the aquarium
before planting will make it easier for you to keep your
arms dry as you work.

Two notched sticks, each about two feet (60 centimeters) long, make good planting tools. Use the
notched end of one stick to hold the plant down and use
the other stick to spread gravel over the plant's roots.

Rooted plants sometimes come loose and float to the surface. Keep replanting them until they finally stay down. You can also plant bunched plants in this way. Simply remove the weight, tear off an inch or two at the bottom of each plant, and push the plant into the gravel.

Arrange your underwater garden so that tall plants, such as eel grass and corkscrew, are planted toward the back of the aquarium. Short plants belong in front, near ornaments. Use plenty of plants in your underwater garden, and remember to remove any plants that die. If you don't, they will pollute the water.

After you have finished planting, lay newspaper on the water's surface to keep the plants in place while you are refilling the tank. Refill the tank by gently pouring back the amount of water that you took away. Pour the water directly on top of the newspaper, and then take the paper away.

PUTTING FISH IN YOUR TANK

During the following four weeks you should add not more than three or four fish to your aquarium. The reason for this is simple. The body wastes of a fish contain a chemical called *ammonia* (uh-MON-ya). This chemical is poisonous and, if allowed to remain in the water, it will kill fish. A filtering system does not remove enough ammonia to keep the water safe, but bacteria do. Bacteria are tiny organisms that use the body waste of fish as food. Thus, they control the amount of ammonia in the tank. About four weeks are required for the bacteria to grow in the tank. During that time, three or four fish give off just enough waste to feed the newly developing bacteria but not enough to poison the water. Filling an aquarium with healthy fish only to have them die within a few weeks is very disappointing. This may happen if you do not give the bacteria in the gravel at least four weeks to grow.

How many fish should you eventually have in your aquarium? If a 10-gallon aquarium is well-planted, filtered, and aerated, it can safely hold 20 to 25 small fish. A 20-gallon tank can hold 20 to 50 fish, depending on their size. If your fish stay at the top of the tank, you may have an overpopulated aquarium. It is far better to have too few fish than too many.

Exotic fish usually are brought home from the pet shop in plastic bags or waxed paper cups. Because any sudden change in temperature is bad for fish, float the containers in your tank for at least 15 minutes before releasing the fish. This will allow the container's water temperature to change to that of the aquarium. To keep foreign pet-shop water out of your aquarium, use a dip net to take your new fish out of their containers and put them in the tank.

To make sure that your fish stay healthy, review this checklist before you start putting together an aquarium: clean the tank and gravel, fill the tank with water, connect the filter and heater, allow the water to age for four or five days, plant the garden, and then add only three or four fish to your aquarium in the first four weeks. If you take all the proper steps, you should have a healthy, balanced aquarium.

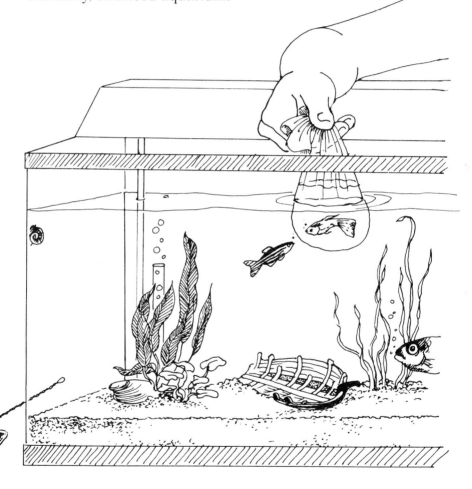

SNAILS

Should you have snails in your tank? Snails add interest to an aquarium, but some have so many babies that they soon take over the tank. Some even eat up the plants.

The apple (or mystery) snail is a good aquarium snail. Because it lays its eggs out of water, usually under the hood of the tank, you can control the snail population by removing the eggs.

This snail can grow to the size of a walnut. Occasionally it will climb to the top of the tank and stick out a funnel-shaped organ through which it takes in a supply of air. It will then sink back to the tank's bottom and lie still for hours. If, however, the snail does not move after one day, it is probably dead. Dead snails pollute the water and make the aquarium smell bad; they should be removed. But healthy snails contribute to the balance of an aquarium by eating algae and spoiled fish food.

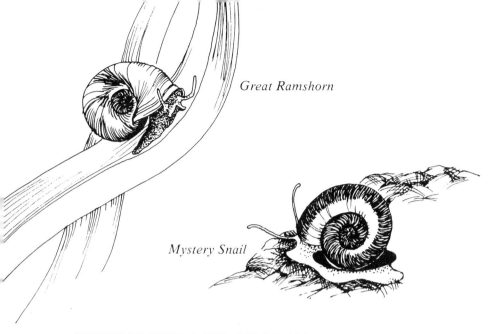

Great Ramshorn

Mystery Snail

KEEPING THE AQUARIUM CLEAN

If you set up your aquarium properly, it should have crystal-clear water and healthy plants and fish. To keep your aquarium this way, you will have to clean it with a dip tube at least once a month. A dip tube is about 18 inches (45 centimeters) long and has a clear plastic bubble near the bottom. To make the tube pick up aquarium debris, hold your finger over its top. Stick the tube into the water until it almost touches the gravel. Take your finger away from the top, and, like magic, the bubble will fill with water. This water carries with it the dirt that has sunk into the gravel. With the full tube still in the water, put your finger back over its top and remove it from the tank. Empty the tube over a container by removing your finger. Repeat this process several times until you have covered most of the bottom of the tank.

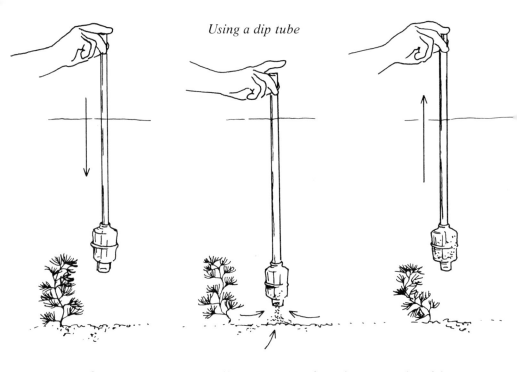

Using a dip tube

Once a month, a gallon or two of tank water should be siphoned off and replaced. Use a rubber tube as a siphon. Move one end of the tube around near the bottom of the tank and let the water and dirt siphon out the other end into a pail. Carefully add new water that has been aged a week; it should be the same temperature as the water in the aquarium. Keep a plastic pail full of water aging somewhere out of sight so that you will have a ready supply. But never replace more than two gallons of aquarium water at a time. Too much new water in the aquarium can be harmful to fish.

If you siphon off dirty water at the beginning of the month and use a dip tube about the middle of the month, your aquarium water should remain clean and sparkling. You should also make regular use of an algae scraper, a long-handled blade for scraping the sides of the aquarium. Even though direct sunlight does not reach your aquarium, some algae will still form on the inside of the glass. A fine grade of steel wool or an aquarium sponge is also good for cleaning glass.

FEEDING YOUR FISH

Fish have many natural sources of food, including algae, large water plants, shrimp and crabs, and the eggs of other fish. And anyone who goes fishing knows that fish also will eat earthworms and insects.

The most popular of all commercial fish foods is the dry flaked food that comes in a can. To feed your fish, simply sprinkle a little of the food on top of the water. Although dry food will constitute most of their diet, you should feed frozen or live food at least once a week.

Frozen food, a mixture of small shrimp and sea scallops, must be stored in the freezing compartment of your refrigerator. To feed frozen food, simply cut off a piece with a knife, place it in a dip net, thaw it under running water, and drop it into your tank.

White worms, brine shrimp, and cut-up earthworms all are live fish foods. You can dig earthworms in your own backyard or buy them from a bait dealer. White worms are sold in pet shops, and come in earth-filled

plastic boxes. They should be kept in a dark, dry place. To feed your fish, place a few worms in a dip net and wash them under a faucet. Then place them in a worm feeder, which is a little floating plastic cup with holes in it. As the worms work their way through the holes, they are eaten by the fish. A worm feeder keeps worms from reaching the tank's bottom before the fish are able to eat them.

Eggs of brine shrimp come in bottles or cans. The eggs look like dried flake food but will hatch into live shrimp when placed in salt water. As long as the eggs are dry, they will keep a long time.

Give your fish only as much food as they can eat in two minutes. Uneaten food will sink to the bottom of the tank, discolor the gravel, and pollute the water. It is better to feed your fish small quantities three times a day than to risk overfeeding them once a day. Because fish will not eat in the dark, be sure to leave the lights on in your aquarium hood after feeding. If you forget to feed your fish once in a while, don't worry—they can go without food for several days.

34

FRESH-WATER EXOTICS

Most fresh-water exotic fish come from warm regions near the equator. Though a few fresh-water exotics are native to Florida or are raised by dealers in the United States, most come from suppliers in Central America, South America, Asia, and Africa. Some fresh-water exotics are live-bearers, and others are egg-layers. Egg-layers are harder to raise in captivity, so if you are interested in breeding fish, try live-bearers first.

Live-Bearers

In planning your first community aquarium, choose fish that are hardy, inexpensive, easy-to-care-for, and friendly. Guppies fit this description exactly. They are live-bearers, native to South America and to the islands of Trinidad and Tobago. Most aquarium guppies, however, are bred in captivity.

Because guppies are good breeders as well as colorful and hardy, they were the first exotics to become popular as aquarium pets. Through selective breeding, guppies have been developed into many beautiful varieties. The inch-long (2.5-centimeter-long) male guppy is spotted with red, blue-green, orange, and black. The female, about half an inch (1.5 centimeters) longer, is a pale silver-grey. A mother guppy bears from six to sixty babies at one time. She can have a new family every four to six weeks. After three months, the babies can have families of their own.

Because guppies are live-bearers, they are easy to breed. The aquarist interested in breeding live-bearers should use a separate tank fitted with a breeding trap. A breeding trap is a plastic box, with small openings, into which the mother is placed when she is ready to have her babies. The holes enable the babies to swim out into the tank, but the mother is too big to fit through these openings. When the young fish have left the trap, the mother should be returned to the community tank.

The purpose of a separate breeding tank for the babies is to allow them to grow up without the danger of being eaten by larger fish. When the babies reach adulthood, they can be transferred to a community tank. But while they are still in the breeding tank, they should be supplied with artificial spawning mops made of nylon wool. These "mops" provide hiding places for the young fish and help keep fine particles of food from sinking to the bottom of the tank.

Breeding different kinds of fancy guppies is a good hobby for the beginning aquarist. Because of selective breeding, today's guppies are a far cry from the drab little creatures of a hundred years ago. The lace guppy has a tail that looks like a fine net. And the veiltail guppy has a long, beautiful tail that resembles a butterfly's wings. An especially fine pair of veiltails can sell for more than a hundred dollars, but less finely bred veiltails cost only a few dollars.

The swordtail ranks after the guppy in popularity. Like the guppy, the swordtail is a hardy fish suited for life in a community tank. It gets its name from the sword-like extension on the male's tail. Since this fish is native to waters in and near Mexico, it is sometimes known as the Mexican swordtail.

The black molly is another hardy live-bearer. Its velvety black appearance in comparison with other fish adds startling contrast to the aquarium. Mollies, which grow to be about two inches (five centimeters) long, feed on algae or small bits of lettuce.

Platys, or moonfish, are popular live-bearers that live well in a community tank. They need much the same care as guppies. A platy may be almost any color—red, orange, gold, metallic blue, or black.

Egg-Layers

Of the egg-laying fish, angel fish are the most beautiful. The adults resemble silver dollars with black stripes. They have large and graceful fins and tails. Because angel fish tend to be scrappy, only a few small specimens should be kept in a community tank. Angel fish are extremely difficult to breed in captivity, as are most egg-layers.

The neon tetra is a small and beautiful fish. Its red and blue markings are so bright thay they almost make the fish look like a neon sign. The neon tetra swims in schools, or groups. Another school fish is the zebra fish,

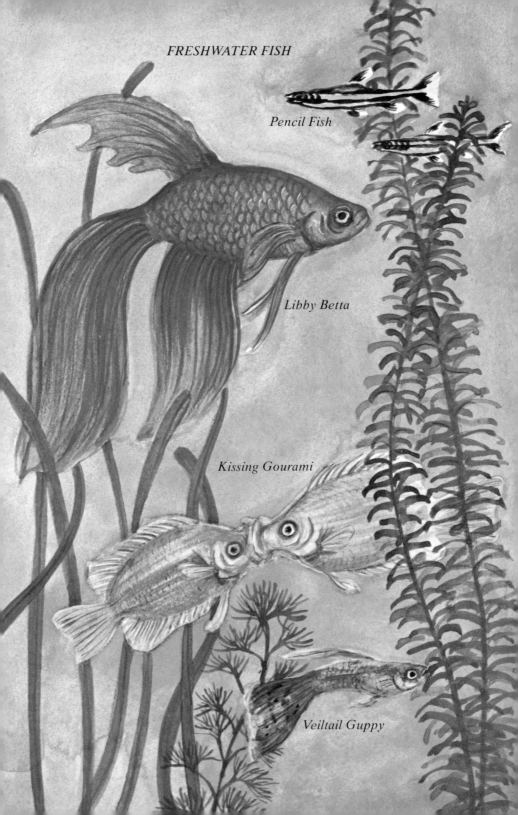

FRESHWATER FISH

Pencil Fish

Libby Betta

Kissing Gourami

Veiltail Guppy

Shubunkin Goldfish

Veiltail Goldfish

Glassfish

Neon Tetra

Wold

which gets its name from its horizontal stripes. The zebra fish is the hardiest of all egg-layers and the easiest to breed.

The beautifully finned fighting fish of Siam, also known as the betta, is quarrelsome, just as its name implies. Male bettas should never be kept in the same tank with each other, because they will probably fight to the death. A male betta preparing for combat flares his gill covers, spreads his fins, and intensifies his colors. He will even do this when he sees himself in a mirror held against the aquarium glass.

In spite of his war-like spirit, the male betta builds a bubble nest for the female's eggs and takes care of the young. He can live nicely in a community aquarium, but will probably be troublesome when protecting his babies in their bubble nest.

Another bubble-nest builder is the dwarf gourami (guh-RAH-me). Because of its size, it is a good fish to have in a small aquarium. This shy, peace-loving fish is the most colorful of all the gouramis. Its silver sides are striped with red and blue, and the male has a larger patch of blue on its underside. The higher the water temperature, the more intense the gourami's colors will be.

The kissing gourami is so named because of the shape of its mouth when it eats and sucks up debris. Gouramis occasionally bump into each other with their "puckered lips" and look as if they are kissing.

Catfish are scavengers, which means they eat things other fish leave. They are good fish to have in an aquarium because they help keep the tank clean. With their little "whiskers," they turn over and inspect pieces of gravel in their search for food.

Whether you choose egg-layers or live-bearers, it is a good idea to buy exotic fish in pairs. The male and female are good company for each other and probably will go through their spawning, or mating, rituals, even in a community tank.

With hundreds of different exotic fish from which to choose, you will select each of your fish for different reasons: bright coloring, perhaps, an odd shape, or unusual habits. Along with the common favorites, you may want to buy the glassfish, whose entire skeleton is visible through its transparent skin; the hatchet fish, which is shaped like a hatchet; the clown barb, which looks as if it is dressed in circus clothing; or the pencil fish, which is long and thin, as its name implies.

Goldfish

Goldfish are egg-laying fish native to the waters of temperate regions. They little resemble their olive-drab ancestors, which swam the streams of China 1,500 years ago. Through selective breeding, the Chinese, and later the Japanese, developed these small members of the carp family into the colorful, fancy-finned beauties we know today.

SALTWATER FISH

Clown Fish

Black Angel Fish

Sea Horse

Queen Angel Fish

Brain Coral

Sea Urchin

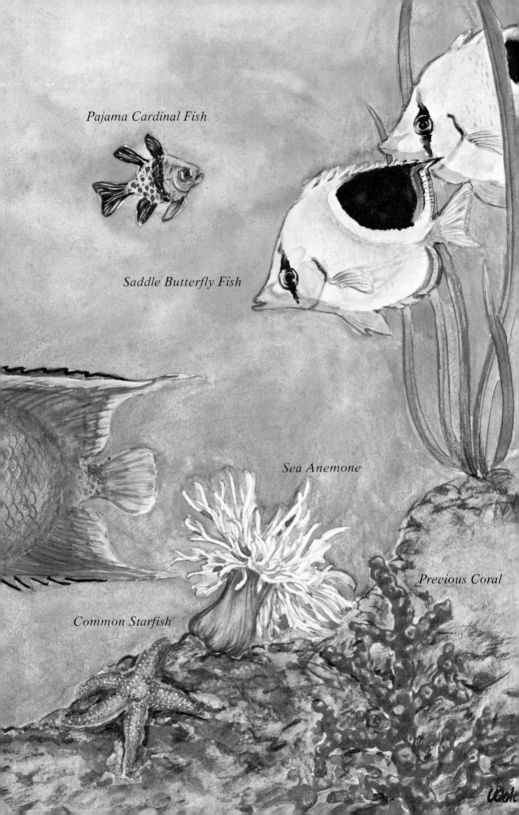

Pajama Cardinal Fish

Saddle Butterfly Fish

Sea Anemone

Precious Coral

Common Starfish

Goldfish were brought to the United States more than a hundred years ago. Since then, they have grown in popularity, and number about 75 million. They are hardy aquarium favorites that also can survive in outdoor streams and pools.

Goldfish are divided into three general groups according to the appearance of their scales. Scaled goldfish have shiny, colorful scales that look like burnished metal. These fish are referred to as "metallics" or "scaled metallics." The common goldfish, the kind found most often in home aquariums, belongs to the metallic group. Due to selective breeding, common goldfish come in varying shades of gold. These attractive fish are not expensive, and they are ideal for beginning aquarists.

The second group of goldfish, known as "matts," are scaleless and are not as shiny as the metallics. The third group, "calicoes," result from mating matts with metallics. They have patches of different colors on their bodies.

Fancy goldfish, with their colorful body patterns, unusual body shapes, or elaborate tail and fin formations, are more expensive than common goldfish. Among the fancy varieties is the shubunkin (shoe-BOON-kin), whose name means "autumn brocade" in Japanese. It is a fancy calico goldfish with large fins. Though no two shubunkins are exactly alike, most are mottled with blue, orange, red, yellow, and black.

The comet goldfish is a deep red metallic with a long tail and large fins. Because it is able to stand extremes in temperature, it can survive in outdoor pools the year around, even in temperate climates.

The fantail goldfish, also a metallic, is an inexpensive, hardy fish with a double tail fin.

The veiltail has long, flowing fins that resemble veils or lacy curtains. There are veiltails in all three groups of goldfish.

The telescope goldfish has pop eyes, which give it a slightly grotesque appearance. When planning an aquarium for telescope goldfish, do not use decorative rocks and ornaments. Telescope goldfish may damage their protruding eyes on such objects. Though telescopes are the most difficult of all goldfish to raise, the black moor telescope is popular because of its black, velvety appearance.

The lionhead is a poor swimmer because of its short body and misshapen head. Its head looks as if it is covered with a growth somewhat resembling a lion's mane. The oranda has a veiltail in addition to a warty looking head. Both orandas and lionheads are expensive, and they are difficult goldfish to raise.

All goldfish need plenty of oxygen. A 20-gallon aerated and filtered tank can hold up to 10 small goldfish. Because goldfish originated in temperate climates, the water temperature of their tank or pool should be between 50 and 68 degrees Fahrenheit (10 to 20 degrees

Celsius). Underwater plants that grow best at these temperatures are anacharis, sagittaria, labelia, and cabomba. Goldfish can survive on flake food, but their diets should be supplemented with some frozen and live foods.

Goldfish are egg-layers, and therefore difficult to breed in a home aquarium. Out of the thousands of eggs that are laid, only a small proportion hatch. In order for these babies to survive, water conditions must be nearly perfect.

SALT-WATER AQUARIUMS

Salt-water aquariums open up a whole new world of sea creatures that you otherwise would see only by visiting the seashore or a public aquarium. If you ever have pondered how a starfish walks or if you marvel at the beauty of coral, perhaps a salt-water aquarium is for you.

Before starting a salt-water aquarium, you should first familiarize yourself with fresh-water tropicals and goldfish. Caring for these fish will give you the experience you need to care for a salt-water, or marine, aquarium. Marine creatures are quite expensive, and a beginning aquarist probably would have trouble keeping them alive.

A tank to be used for salt water should not have any metal parts, because salt water rusts and corrodes metals, including stainless steel.

Before you set up the aquarium, you should clean the tank and all the equipment to be placed inside it with a brine, or salt, solution. To make this solution, fill the aquarium with tap water and add three tablespoons of table salt for each gallon of water in the aquarium. Soak the undergravel filter, floating thermometer, heater, rocks, coral, and ornaments in this brine solution for three days. The salt water should destroy any bacteria or insects on the equipment. After the three-

day soak, thoroughly rinse all the equipment in fresh water. Never use soap in your aquarium; even the smallest trace of soap can be deadly to marine life.

Setting up a marine aquarium is similar to setting up an aquarium for tropical fish. The big difference, of course, is that you must use salt water rather than fresh water.

Even if you live near an ocean, you should make your own salt water. Natural sea water is sometimes polluted and can contain harmful bacteria. To make your own sea water, mix fresh water with the special salts sold in pet shops. Be sure to follow the directions that come with each package of salt. They will tell you in what proportions you should mix the salts and water. If the tap water in your home is full of minerals, dissolve the salts in distilled water or water that has gone through a water softener.

One extra piece of equipment you will need for a marine aquarium is a hydrometer to measure the salinity, or saltiness, of the water. The hydrometer in a marine tank should read about 1.025. If the salinity exceeds 1.030, fresh water should be added to the tank. If the reading is less than 1.020, more salt is needed. Ask the experts at your pet shop how to maintain the proper salinity.

Because your marine aquarium has salt water, you must use only marine plants in it. Marine plants are difficult to grow and will not grow at all in tanks that

do not have under-gravel filters. The reason for this is that the roots of marine plants give off gases that must be filtered out. A good under-gravel filter, then, and plenty of aeration are necessary for a marine aquarium. The water temperature should be between 70 and 80 degrees Fahrenheit (21 and 27 degrees Celsius).

The best ornaments for a marine aquarium are pieces of cured coral and cured clam shells. Shells from baby giant clams, known as *tridacna* (trih-DAHK-nuh), are best. They are easy to clean, and they provide snug hiding places for timid fish and animals.

Shells, rocks, or coral you find along the beach contain animal life and bacteria that could poison your aquarium water. You should, therefore, cure these

natural ornaments by soaking them in fresh water for about three weeks. Then dry them in the sun for about two weeks. Many marine aquariums that fail do so because of improperly cured shells and coral.

MARINE CREATURES

The creatures that can live in a marine tank vary from the exceptionally beautiful queen angel fish to the curious-looking sea horse, which is also a fish. To keep such marine creatures alive, you must create exactly the right conditions in your tank. You must always keep an eye on the temperature and the salinity of the water, and you must feed your pets a variety of good food. In addition to dry food, they should be fed a good supply of fresh food such as frozen shrimp. Lean beef, finely chopped, is an excellent supplement. Pieces of earthworm are also good.

50

The sea horse has long enjoyed an admiring public because of its unusual antics and horsey appearance. Certain species grow to 12 inches (30 centimeters) in length. The dwarf sea horse, however, is best for home salt-water aquariums.

The sea horse is not a good swimmer, but it has a strong tail with which it can grasp coral or plants. When setting up an aquarium for sea horses, be sure to put in sea fans or pieces of coral for "hitching posts."

An interesting fact about sea horse reproduction is that the female lays her eggs in a pouch in the male's belly. The male then incubates the eggs for 40 to 50 days until the young are "born." Baby sea horses generally do not survive in home aquariums.

The pygmy pipefish is a relative of the dwarf sea horse. When fully grown, it looks like a finger-sized piece of pipe. Both pipefish and sea horses eat only live foods. Brine shrimp hatched from eggs will satisfy these fussy eaters. But guard against overfeeding, which will pollute the water.

The lionfish, sometimes called the turkeyfish or featherfish, has spiny fins that stick out like feathers. Some of its spines are capable of injecting a poisonous fluid into prey. This fluid stuns small fish long enough for them to be swallowed by the lionfish. If kept in aquariums by themselves, lionfish should stay healthy for at least a year. At one time, lionfish cost as much as $300 each, but now they sell for about $15.

The clownfish's bright orange and white stripes make it resemble a clown's costume. This small creature is also known as the anemone (uh-NEH-muh-nee) fish because its natural home is among the poisonous arms of the sea anemone. It is one of the few fish immune to the anemone's poison. Clownfish can live as long as five years. They are good fish to have in a community salt-water aquarium.

Several kinds of angel fish are popular, and among the most popular is the queen angel fish. Some fish fanciers think this fish the most beautiful in the world. Its lovely colors are the brightest when the fish is about two inches (five centimeters) long. Other exotic angel fish include the blue, black, and French angel fish. Many angel fish, however, are too delicate and too expensive for the home aquarist.

Other favorites of salt-water aquarists are butterfly fish, sergeant majors, cardinal fish, marine jewel fish, neon gobies, and demoiselles.

Some salt-water enthusiasts may be more interested in creatures that scuttle or lurk on the sea's bottom than in creatures that swim. In that case, marine snails, crabs, and shrimp make interesting pets, and can thrive

in a properly set up salt-water aquarium. Keeping live coral, starfish, and sea anemones is a much more difficult task, but it can be done. And it promises to present a real challenge to the serious-minded aquarist.

If you live by an ocean, you can have the fun of collecting your own specimens. Otherwise you can obtain sea animals from special pet shops or mail-order marine supply houses.

The world of underwater plants and animals becomes a little less mysterious when we keep aquariums. We can better understand Nature's delicate balance between plants and animals and between animals and other animals by keeping aquariums. And with the world's increasing reliance on the sea for food, the study of underwater life becomes ever more important.

INDEX

aerator, 14
aging the water, 22-23, 32
algae, 18, 33
algae scraper, 33
ammonia, 27-28
angel fish: fresh-water, 37; salt-water, 52
apple snail, 30
aquarist, 8
aquarium crystal paint, 19
aquarium hoods, 18-19
aquarium keeping as hobby, 7
aquarium stands, 18

bacteria, importance of, 28
balance of underwater life, 8, 30
betta, 40
black molly, 37
bony fish, 10
breeding tank, 36
breeding trap, 36
bubble nest, 40
bunched plants, 24, 27

calico (goldfish), 44
carbon dioxide, 13
cartilaginous fish, 10
cartilaginous skeletons, 10
catfish, 41
chemicals in water, 23
cleaning the tank, 21, 31, 47-48
clown barb, 41
clownfish (anemone fish), 52
cold-bloodedness, 10, 19
curing of shells, 49-50

dip tube, 31, 33

egg-layers, 10, 37-41, 46
evolution of fish, 7
"exotic fish," definition of, 9

fighting fish of Siam, 40
filter, 14-15, 21, 49
floating plants, 24
fluorescent lights, 18
flying fish, 11
food for fish, 33-34, 46, 50
fresh-water exotic fish, 16, 35-46

gills, 11, 12
glass fish, 41
goldfish, 41-46
gourami, 40
gravel, 21
guppies, 35-36

hatchet fish, 41
hydrometer, 48

lateral line system, 12
lionfish, 51
live-bearers, 10, 35-37

mail-order marine supply houses, 53
marine aquarium, 47-50
marine plants, 48-49
matt (goldfish), 44
metallic (goldfish), 44

nature of fish, 9-12
neon tetra, 37

ornaments, 22, 49-50
oxygen, importance of, 12-13, 14

pencil fish, 41
planting tools, 26
plants, 24-27, 46
platy, 37
pollution of tank water, 27, 30, 34,
    48, 49, 51
pygmy pipefish, 51

respiration, 13
rooted plants, 24, 27

salinity, 48, 50
salt-water exotic fish, 16, 51-52
salt water (for marine tanks), 48
scavengers, 30, 41

sea as cradle of life, 7
sea horse, 51
selective breeding, 35, 41
shells, 49-50
siphon, 32-33
snail eggs, 30
spawning, 41
spawning mops, 36
swordtail, 37

tanks: price of, 16; salt-water, 47;
    size of, 17, 28, 45
thermostat-heater, 19-20
tridacna, 49
"tropical fish," definition of, 8-9

walking fish, 11
worm feeder, 34

zebra fish, 37-40

You and Your Pet:

AQUARIUM PETS

BIRDS

CATS

DOGS

HORSES

RODENTS AND RABBITS

TERRARIUM PETS

We specialize in publishing quality books for young people. For a complete list please write

LERNER PUBLICATIONS COMPANY

241 First Avenue North, Minneapolis, Minnesota 55401